G000022612

The
Ten
Commandments

The Ten Commandments

Exodus 19-20:20

Adapted from the
King James Bible

Ariel Books

**Andrews McMeel
Publishing**

Kansas City

Photography © 1998 Catherine Gehm

www.andrewsmcmeel.com

ISBN: 0-8362-6808-3
Library of Congress Catalog Card Number: 98-84249

19

*I*N THE third month, when the children of Israel were gone forth out of the land of Egypt, the same day came they *into* the wilderness of Sinai.

2

For they were departed
from Rephidim, and
were come *to* the desert
of Sinai, and had
pitched in the
wilderness; and there
Israel camped before
the mount.

3

AND MOSES WENT UP
UNTO GOD, AND THE
LORD CALLED UNTO
HIM OUT OF THE
MOUNTAIN, SAYING,
THUS SHALT THOU SAY
TO THE HOUSE OF
JACOB, AND TELL THE
CHILDREN OF ISRAEL;

THE TEN COMMANDMENTS

4

YE HAVE SEEN WHAT I
DID UNTO THE
EGYPTIANS, AND *HOW*
I BARE YOU ON EAGLES'
WINGS, AND BROUGHT
YOU UNTO MYSELF.

5

Now therefore, if ye will obey my voice indeed, and keep my covenant, then ye shall be a peculiar treasure unto me above all people: for all the earth *is* mine:

THE TEN COMMANDMENTS

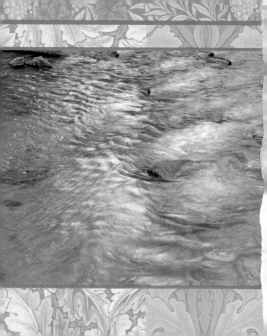

6

AND YE SHALL BE
UNTO ME A KINGDOM
OF PRIESTS, AND AN
HOLY NATION. THESE
ARE THE WORDS
WHICH THOU SHALT
SPEAK UNTO THE
CHILDREN OF ISRAEL.

17

7

And Moses came and
called for the elders
of the people, and
aid before their faces
all these words
which the LORD
commanded him.

8

AND ALL THE PEOPLE
answered together,
and said, All that the
LORD hath spoken we
will do. AND MOSES
returned the words of
the people unto
the LORD.

9

And the LORD said unto
Moses, Lo, I come unto
thee in a thick cloud,
that the people may hear
when I speak with thee,
and believe thee for ever.
And Moses told the
words of the people unto
the LORD.

10

And the LORD said unto Moses, Go unto the people, and sanctify them today and tomorrow, and let them wash their clothes.

11

And be ready against the third day: for the third day the LORD will come down in the sight of all the people upon mount Sinai.

12

And thou shalt set bounds unto the people round about, saying, Take heed to yourselves, *that ye* go *not* up into the mount, or touch the border of it: whosoever toucheth the mount shall be surely put to death:

THE TEN COMMANDMENTS

13

THERE SHALL NOT AN HAND
TOUCH IT, BUT HE SHALL SURELY
BE STONED, OR SHOT THROUGH;
WHETHER *IT BE* BEAST OR MAN,
IT SHALL NOT LIVE: WHEN THE
TRUMPET SOUNDETH LONG,
THEY SHALL COME UP
TO THE MOUNT.

31

14

AND MOSES WENT DOWN
FROM THE MOUNT
UNTO THE PEOPLE, AND
SANCTIFIED THE PEOPLE;
AND THEY WASHED
THEIR CLOTHES.

15
And he said unto the
people, Be ready against
the third day: come not
at *your* wives.

16

And it came to pass on the third day in the morning, that there were thunders and lightnings, and a thick cloud upon the mount, and the voice of the trumpet exceeding loud; so that all the people that *was* in the camp trembled.

17

AND MOSES BROUGHT
FORTH THE PEOPLE OUT OF
THE CAMP TO MEET WITH
GOD; AND THEY STOOD AT
THE NETHER PART OF
THE MOUNT.

And mount Sinai was altogether on a smoke, because the LORD descended upon it in fire: and the smoke thereof ascended as the smoke of a furnace, and the whole mount quaked greatly.

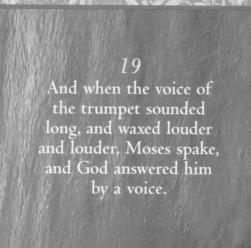

19

And when the voice of
the trumpet sounded
long, and waxed louder
and louder, Moses spake,
and God answered him
by a voice.

20

And the LORD came down upon
mount Sinai, on top of the mount:
and the LORD called Moses *up* to
the top of the mount; and Moses
went up.

_21_

AND THE LORD SAID
UNTO MOSES, GO
DOWN, CHARGE THE
PEOPLE, LEST THEY
BREAK THROUGH UNTO
THE LORD TO GAZE,
AND MANY OF THEM
PERISH.

THE TEN COMMANDMENTS

22

And let the priests also, which come near to the LORD, sanctify them-selves, lest the LORD break forth upon them.

23

And Moses said unto
the LORD, The people
cannot come up to
mount Sinai: for thou
chargedst us, saying, Set
bounds about the mount,
and sanctify it.

THE TEN COMMANDMENTS

24

AND THE LORD SAID UNTO
HIM, AWAY, GET THEE
DOWN, AND THOU SHALT
COME UP, THOU, AND
AARON WITH THEE: BUT
LET NOT THE PRIESTS AND
THE PEOPLE BREAK
THROUGH TO COME UP
UNTO THE LORD, LEST HE
BREAK FORTH UPON THEM.

25

So Moses went down
unto the people, and
spake unto them.

20

ND GOD SPAKE all these
words, saying,

2   I *am* the LORD thy God, which
have brought thee out of the land of
Egypt, out of the house of bondage.

THE TEN COMMANDMENTS

3

Thou shalt have
no other gods
before me.

4

THOU SHALT NOT MAKE
UNTO THEE ANY GRAVEN
IMAGE, OR ANY LIKENESS
OF ANY THING THAT *IS*
IN HEAVEN ABOVE, OR
THAT *IS* IN THE EARTH
BENEATH, OR THAT *IS* IN
THE WATER UNDER
THE EARTH:

THE TEN COMMANDMENTS

5

THOU SHALT NOT BOW
DOWN THYSELF TO THEM,
NOR SERVE THEM: FOR I
THE LORD THY GOD AM A
JEALOUS GOD, VISITING THE
INIQUITY OF THE FATHERS
UPON THE CHILDREN UNTO
THE THIRD AND FOURTH
GENERATION OF THEM
THAT HATE ME;

6

AND SHOWING MERCY
UNTO THOUSANDS OF
THEM THAT LOVE ME,
AND KEEP MY
COMMANDMENTS.

7

Thou shalt not take the
name of the LORD thy
God in vain; for the
LORD will not hold him
guiltless that taketh his
name in vain.

THE TEN COMMANDMENTS

8

REMEMBER THE
SABBATH DAY,
TO KEEP IT HOLY.

THE TEN COMMANDMENTS

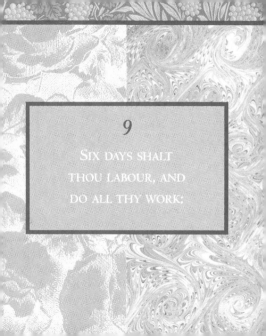

9

Six days shalt thou labour, and do all thy work:

12

HONOUR THY FATHER
AND THY MOTHER:
THAT THY DAYS MAY
BE LONG UPON THE
LAND WHICH THE
LORD THY GOD
GIVETH THEE.

13

Thou shalt not kill.

14

Thou shalt not commit
adultery.

15

THOU
SHALT NOT
STEAL.

10

But the seventh day *is* the sabbath of the Lord thy God: *in it* thou shalt not do any work, thou, nor thy son, nor thy daughter, thy manservant, nor thy maidservant, nor thy cattle, nor thy stranger that *is* within thy gates:

11

For *in* six days the
LORD made heaven and
earth, the sea, and all
that in them *is*, and
rested the seventh day:
wherefore the LORD
blessed the sabbath day,
and hallowed it.

16
Thou shalt not bear
false witness against thy
neighbour.

17

THOU SHALT NOT COVET
THY NEIGHBOUR'S HOUSE,
THOU SHALT NOT COVET
THY NEIGHBOUR'S WIFE,
NOR HIS MANSERVANT, NOR
HIS MAIDSERVANT, NOR HIS
OX, NOR HIS ASS, NOR ANY
THING THAT *IS* THY
NEIGHBOUR'S.

18

AND ALL THE PEOPLE SAW
THE THUNDERINGS, AND
THE LIGHTNINGS, AND THE
NOISE OF THE TRUMPET,
AND THE MOUNTAIN
SMOKING: AND WHEN THE
PEOPLE SAW *IT*, THEY
REMOVED, AND STOOD
AFAR OFF.

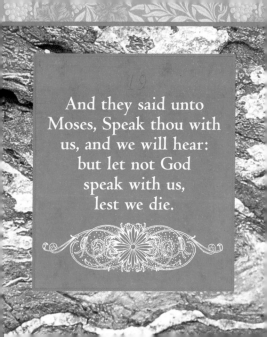

And they said unto
Moses, Speak thou with
us, and we will hear:
but let not God
speak with us,
lest we die.

AND MOSES SAID UNTO
THE PEOPLE, FEAR NOT:
FOR GOD IS COME TO
PROVE YOU, AND THAT HIS
FEAR MAY BE BEFORE YOUR
FACES, THAT YE SIN NOT.

Composed in Centaur and Lucia with
QuarkXPress™ and Adobe® Illustrator™
on the Macintosh computer

Book design and composition by
JUDITH STAGNITTO ABBATE
of Abbate Design
Doylestown, Pennsylvania